USING EXPOSURE THERAPY TO TREAT ANXIETY PROBLEMS

CLYDE M. FELDMAN, Ph.D.

A Clyde Feldman, Ph. D. Publication

USING EXPOSURE THERAPY TO TREAT ANXIETY PROBLEMS

Copyright © 2012 Clyde M. Feldman, Ph.D.

All rights reserved.

Printed in the United States of America

All rights reserved. No part of this book may be reproduced or transmitted in any form or by any means, electronic or mechanical, including photocopying, recording, or by any information storage and retrieval system, without permission in writing from the publisher.

*****

Formatting By Debora Lewis
www.arenapublishing.org

ISBN-13: 978-1480063150

ISBN-10: 1480063150

USING EXPOSURE THERAPY TO TREAT ANXIETY PROBLEMS

(SYSTEMATIC DESENSITIZATION)

A STEP-BY-STEP, CLINICAL GUIDE TO USING THE EXPOSURE THERAPY PROCEDURE FOR SIX TYPES OF ANXIETY. INCLUDES WORKSHEETS AND SCRIPTS FOR UNDERSTANDING HOW ANXIETY PROBLEMS WORKS, AND FOR USING RELAXATION, COPING SKILLS, AND POSITIVE COUNTER-THOUGHTS AND IMAGES.

FOR COUNSELORS, THERAPISTS, AND BEHAVIORAL HEALTH PRACTITIONERS.

CLYDE M. FELDMAN, PH.D.

LICENSED MARRIAGE AND FAMILY THERAPIST
LICENSED PROFESSIONAL COUNSELOR
CERTIFIED NLP MASTER PRACTITIONER

TUCSON, AZ,
(520)-326-6060,
E-MAIL: CMFELDMAN@AOL.COM
WEB: COUNSELINGTOOLSTHATWORK.COM

CONTENTS

SECTION 1:   HOW ANXIETY WORKS.. 1

                A MODEL OF THE FACTORS WHICH LEAD TO
                AND MAINTAIN ANXIETY PROBLEMS........................ 2

                DESCRIPTION OF THE MODEL OF ANXIETY.................... 3

SECTION 2:   THE EXPOSURE THERAPY STEPS........................... 7

                OVERVIEW OF THE EXPOSURE THERAPY STEPS............. 8

       STEP 1:   GET DETAILED INFORMATION ABOUT THE ANXIETY
                       PROBLEM.. 9

       STEP 2:   CHOOSE A TARGET TYPE FOR EXPOSURE............. 12

       STEP 3:   IDENTIFY THE IRRATIONAL, CATASTROPHIC, DISTORTED
                       THOUGHTS, PICTURES, BELIEFS, ASSUMPTIONS,
                       AND EXPECTATIONS................................... 14

       STEP 4:   DEVELOP BEHAVIORAL SKILLS FOR PHYSICALLY AND
                       MENTALLY RELAXING................................ 18

       STEP 5:   IDENTIFY AND DEVELOP COGNITIVE RESOURCES
                       AND COPING SKILLS................................. 20

       STEP 6:   DEVELOP A GRADED HIERARCHY....................... 25

       STEP 7:   LEARN THE SUDs SCALE TO KEEP TRACK OF THE
                     LEVEL OF ANXIETY.................................. 26

       STEP 8:   OPTIONAL RELAXATION EXERCISE..................... 27

       STEP 9:   START IMAGINAL EXPOSURE........................... 28

      STEP 10:   IN-VIVO EXPOSURE.................................. 30

SECTION 3:	CLINICAL TOOLS.. 31

- ⇨ THE ANXIETY INVENTORY................................... 32
- ⇨ IDENTIFYING CURRENT TRIGGERS WORKSHEET........... 38
- ⇨ TECHNIQUES FOR ELICITING A SPECIFIC BODY SENSATION AS A TARGET................................. 39
- ⇨ ANXIETY REACTION &TRAUMA REACTION WORKSHEETS.... 41
- ⇨ PROGRESSIVE MUSCLE RELAXATION SCRIPTS............. 43
- ⇨ PASSIVE MUSCLE RELAXATION SCRIPTS.................. 52
- ⇨ BREATHING TECHNIQUES SCRIPTS........................ 56
- ⇨ CREATING A SPECIAL PLACE SCRIPTS..................... 59
- ⇨ BEACH AND FOREST SPECIAL PLACE SCRIPTS............. 61
- ⇨ 16 THINGS TO ASK YOURSELF ABOUT YOUR THOUGHTS, BELIEFS, ASSUMPTIONS, AND EXPECTATIONS.............. 63
- ⇨ POSITIVE COUNTER-STATEMENTS AND PICTURES WORKSHEET FOR REDUCING ANXIETY...................... 65
- ⇨ GRADED HIERARCHY WORKSHEET......................... 66

SECTION 4:	BOOK REFERENCES ON EXPOSURE THERAPY................ 69

SECTION 1:

HOW ANXIETY WORKS

A MODEL OF THE FACTORS WHICH LEAD TO AND MAINTAIN ANXIETY PROBLEMS

BIOLOGICAL VULNERABILITY

- Tendency To Be More Emotionally Reactive
- Biochemical Imbalances or Deficits

↓

EMOTIONAL INSECURITIES

- Cautious, Dangerous World View
- Feeling Rejected, Neglected
- Poor Social Skills

↓

FALSE ALARM

ANXIOUS OVER-REACTION TO EVENTS AND SITUATIONS WHICH ARE NOT TRULY DANGEROUS

↓

LEARNED RESPONSES THAT MAINTAIN OR INCREASE THE FALSE ALARM

- Anxious Self-Talk, Mental Pictures, and Beliefs
- Avoidance of the Feared Situations or Objects
- Compulsive Behaviors
- Partner Is <u>Non</u>-Supportive or <u>Overly</u>-Supportive

DESCRIPTION OF THE MODEL OF ANXIETY

Although each person's anxiety problem has a different origin, there is a general model about how and why anxiety problems start and what tends to maintain or even increase them. The model on the previous page is based on extensive research by David Barlow and his colleagues (see references p. 70). This model of anxiety is explained below.

BIOLOGICAL VULNERABILITY

- Tendency To Be More Emotionally Reactive

Anxiety problems are associated with an inherited vulnerability, tendency, or predisposition towards: (1) "nervousness", (2) a more "excitable" autonomic nervous system, (3) a stronger attention to "threat", and (4) a tendency to withdraw from unfamiliar situations. That "tendency" appears to be activated under stressful situations. A person is four times more likely to have an anxiety problem if a first-degree relative has it. This is most true for OCD, panic, and specific phobias. It is less true for generalized anxiety disorder and PTSD.

- Biochemical Imbalances or Deficits

Anxiety problems are associated with imbalances or deficits in neurotransmitter levels and/or hormone levels. Also some individuals may have a central nervous system monitor that is oversensitive to "suffocation" via elevated levels of carbon dioxide (can make people have attack with increased levels of carbon dioxide).

EMOTIONAL INSECURITIES

- Cautious, Dangerous World View

Anxiety problems are associated with parents or family members communicating an overly cautious view of the world to a child ("Don't go out in rain, you'll catch cold", "Don't play in dirt, you'll get germs"). *Be very careful* messages encourage a view of the world as a dangerous place where one's exploration and risk-taking should be restricted.

- **Feeling Rejected, Neglected**

Anxiety problems are associated with childhood neglect, rejection, abandonment, abuse, shame, guilt, as well as overtly negative experiences via divorce, deaths, or illness. These types of experience can create feeling of emotional dependency in response to insecurity.

- **Poor Social Skills**

Anxiety problems are associated with poorer communication skills (i.e., talks less, self-discloses less, expresses opinions less, seems less enthusiastic and less genuine), poorer assertiveness skills, and being less able to read others and their emotions.

↓

FALSE ALARM

ANXIOUS OVER-REACTION TO EVENTS AND SITUATIONS
WHICH ARE NOT TRULY DANGEROUS

↓

LEARNED RESPONSES THAT MAINTAIN OR INCREASE THE FALSE ALARM

- **Anxious Self-Talk, Beliefs, and Mental Pictures**

Anxious individuals create a wide range of anxious self-talk, anxious mental images, and anxious beliefs making dysfunctional assumptions, presumptions, expectations, and anticipations about how likely the next occurrence will be, how catastrophic the outcome will be, and how unable they will be to cope with and manage the situation, event, or object.

- ## Avoidance of the Feared Situations or Objects

Avoidance tends to get increasingly reinforced and strengthened because it reduces anxiety, at least initially. Avoidance also serves to keep the person from realizing that their reaction is a "False Alarm" rather than being valid and necessary ("True Alarm").

(Patterns of Self-talk and Avoidance)

The common ways in which self-talk/mental pictures/beliefs and avoidance operate with anxiety problems are described below.

PANIC: Self-talk validates the belief that the physical sensations are dangerous or life threatening thereby getting the person more and more panicky (hyperventilate, etc.). The person anticipates future attacks and the fear of having another attack becomes their biggest fear. Avoidance of situations where a person can't get help easily or would feel humiliated can ultimately limit their ability to function normally and may lead to Agoraphobic behavior.

GENERALIZED ANXIETY DISORDER: Worry increases stress which decreases the person's ability to cope with stressors. It may also lower their positive sense of self which only aggravates the more core and global fears underlying GAD such as fear of failure, rejection, not being in control, or not being good enough or perfect. Avoidance is often related to worrying in such a way as to distract oneself or "worry shift" before one can fully evaluate the realistic outcome or their realistic ability to cope with the outcome.

SOCIAL ANXIETY: Self-talk leads to increased levels of anxiety which then leads to doing or saying things that ultimately are embarrassing or socially awkward (e.g., forget during public speaking). Avoidance (e.g., parties, dating) never gives the person a chance to develop and practice needed social skills and to gain needed confidence.

SPECIFIC PHOBIA: Self-talk validates the belief that feared situations are too dangerous to manage and that the person doesn't have the ability to cope or handle such intense stimuli. Avoidance makes it unlikely that the person will ever: (1) confront the situation in order to know it is not inherently dangerous, and (2) develop the skills and coping abilities to handle feared situations.

PTSD: Self-talk increases the likelihood that the person will re-traumatize themselves by re-experiencing all the original symptoms in response to more and more generalized triggers. Avoiding aspects of situations that remind the person of the trauma can contribute to the triggers never becoming neutralized and contributing to a belief that "I'll never get over this".

OCD: Self-talk validates that the obsessions will come true if the person doesn't do something to stop them AND validates that the obsessions cannot be gotten rid of or reduced by ordinary means but rather require compulsions to neutralize them. Also, that the person is not able to control of their own thoughts and images. Avoidance in OCD is replaced with compulsive behavior. As with avoidance, enacting the compulsion makes it unlikely that the person will ever experience that the obsessions are NOT valid and will NOT come true.

- ## Compulsive Behaviors (See OCD)

- ## Relationship Responses

NON-SUPPORTIVE: These partners doesn't take the problem seriously or become irate, resentful, critical, or intolerant of the problem. (Examples: Fear of flying partner becomes irate and resentful that plans must be changed or cancelled; Panic partner sees that treatment for panic makes little difference and becomes fed-up, overtly critical, and intolerant which leaves person feeling more fearful, alone, and depressed; OCD partner is tired of the person's constant need for reassurance about contamination until partner stops caring; OCD partner has to wait an extra hour for person to re-check or re-wash; OCD family can't have certain foods cause person refuses to buy or cook them; GAD partner begins to stop caring and withdraws which leaves person feeling more insecure and worried).

OVERLY-SUPPORTIVE: These partners allow the problem person to become too dependent or reliant on them. (Examples: Panic partner becomes over-involved and indulges partner about eating more at home, not going out to movies, etc., which reinforces the agoraphobia and indirectly encourages person to give up more responsibilities; Social anxiety partner takes over by doing all the talking at parties, making excuses for him not giving the presentation, not having to eat in public restaurants which reinforces doing less and less socially; PTSD partner is very understanding about the residual affects of a sexual assault and will not pressure or push her to be sexual or close or express her feelings which ultimately decreases their intimacy level).

SECTION 2:

THE EXPOSURE THERAPY STEPS

Clyde M. Feldman, Ph.D.

OVERVIEW OF EXPOSURE THERAPY

Exposure Therapy, and its earlier version Systematic Desensitization, was developed from within Behavior Therapy and Cognitive-Behavior Therapy. It is one of the most "evidence-based" technologies in use in the psychotherapy field today. It has been successfully used for over 40 years with a wide range of anxiety-based problems and disorders, including Specific Phobias, Generalized Anxiety, Panic, Post-Traumatic Stress, Social Anxiety, and Obsessive Compulsive disorder.

There Are Three Primary Principles Operating in Exposure Therapy. They Are:

1. When people are "exposed" (in real life or in one's imagination) to a feared situation without the expected negative consequences actually happening, they naturally begin to "desensitize" to it (i.e., stay calmer, more relaxed). Unfortunately, people tend to avoid the feared stimuli and therefore never get a chance to really desensitize to it.

2. Since anxiety about something is also related to a whole range of anxious thinking (what if x happens, catastrophic pictures, etc.), people need to learn to manage and cope with the feared situation by actively changing what they say to themselves, what they picture to themselves, their assumptions, expectations, and beliefs about the feared situation. This anxious thinking and the calmer counter-thinking often relates to issues of:

    - How Likely Something Is to Occur.

    - How Bad or Catastrophic the Outcome Will Be.

    - How Well or Badly They Will Be Able to Tolerate or Cope.

3. Since people are very reluctant to confront their fears and may have very strong anxiety reactions, the feared situation is broken into smaller sub-parts, working on the least anxiety provoking first, and working your way up the to most anxiety provoking last (see step 6 - graded hierarchy).

There Are Ten Steps In The Exposure Therapy Process. They Are Described Next.

STEP 1

GET DETAILED INFORMATION ABOUT THE ANXIETY PROBLEM

1. Gather information from the client about the type(s) of anxiety problem the person is experiencing based on their symptoms or manifestations of it. The Anxiety Inventory referenced below can be filled out by the client. It can be scored by the client, but its preferable that the practitioner score it themselves or in conjunction with the client. Also gather information about the origins of the anxiety problem and the key past events that may have set up an anxiety response to present events and situations.

    ⇨ USE THE ANXIETY INVENTORY (p. 32)

2. Gather information about present triggers that evoke or cue the anxiety response. The worksheet referenced below can help facilitate this process with the client.

    ⇨ USE THE "IDENTIFYING CURRENT TRIGGERS" WORKSHEET (p. 38)

3. In addition to the Anxiety Inventory, a summary of the six types of anxiety problems (based on DSM-IV), with their associated symptoms and kind of feared stimulus are described below. The number in parentheses refers to the percentage of the population estimated to have the disorder.

SPECIFIC PHOBIA (6%)

FEAR OF SPECIFIC NON-SOCIAL OBJECTS OR PLACES (e.g., snakes, bats, rats, spiders, heights, flying, elevators, thunder, lightning, small spaces, needle, injections, the site of blood)

- Excessive or unreasonable fear AND anxiety reaction to specific objects or places that are perceived to be dangerous.

- Must cause significant distress or disruption to your normal routine.

GENERALIZED ANXIETY (5%)

FEAR OF THE CONSEQUENCES OF NEGATIVE LIFE CIRCUMSTANCES AND FEAR THAT YOU WON'T BE ABLE TO COPE (i.e., family, money, work, health)

- Chronic, excessive and unrealistic worrying and anxious feelings about two or more major life circumstances (e.g., about school, career, relationship, child's welfare) much of the time for at least 6 months duration - but NO panic attacks, phobias, or obsession.

- In addition to chronic worry, typically clients are keyed up and tense, irritable, fatigued, have difficulty concentrating, and difficulties with sleep.

- The generalized nature of the anxiety may relate to more core and global fears like failure, rejection, not being in control, not being good enough or perfect enough.

PANIC (5%)

NO SPECIFIC FEARED STIMULUS BUT FEAR OF HAVING MORE UNEXPECTED PANIC ATTACKS IN AWKWARD SITUATIONS

- Panic attacks - recurrent, unexpected, discrete moments of intense anxiety that come on suddenly and last 1 to 10 minutes. Symptoms include accelerated heart rate, chest pain, trembling, sweating, dizziness, light-headedness... also may feel like they are going to die, lose control, or go crazy.

- Ongoing worry and concern about having more attacks, usually at unpredictable times and in unexpected settings, and about the consequences of the attacks (will I be injured, what will people think). When attacks are "cued", the cue is often physical exertion, seeing a crowd, going into an elevator, etc.

- As fear of unexpected attacks increases, some people develop Agoraphobia (fear of "open spaces") or a fear of being in places where you might have a panic attack and escape or help is difficult and/or embarrassing (e.g., driving alone, public transportation, elevators, restaurants, crowds). They avoid or severely limit travel sometimes to the point of being housebound.

    ** Some people have Agoraphobia with no history of panic - (fear of having a heart attack, losing bladder control, etc.)

POST-TRAUMATIC STRESS (4%)
(Develops in 25% of those exposed to trauma - highest among assault victims)

FEAR THAT A PAST TRAUMATIC EVENT WILL HAPPEN AGAIN AND/OR THE OUTCOME WILL OCCUR AGAIN (natural (e.g., earthquake) or man-made disaster (e.g., fire), early abuse, witness and/or experience a violent crime, combat, and car accident)

[Duration must last 1+ months]

- Client experienced a traumatic event involving actual or threatened injury or death to oneself or others close to them AND experienced fear, horror, helplessness.

- Re-experiencing - emotionally and physically - of the traumatic event in the present: (1) in dreams, (2) flashbacks, (3) in response to triggers - objects, types of people, smells, places, time of day, that remind you of it.

- Symptoms of over-arousal including difficulty sleeping, difficulty concentrating, on guard (hypervigilant), easily startled, and easily irritable- brought to anger.

- Avoidance: (1) of people, places, and things that remind one of the event, (2) of conversations about the event, and (3) of thoughts and memories about the event. Sometimes the level of avoidance reaches a point of "disassociation" or shutting down of emotional and relational reactions, tuning out, "numbness".

SOCIAL ANXIETY (3%)

FEAR OF SOCIAL SITUATIONS (e.g.,public speaking, dating, parties, social and family gatherings, using public restrooms, taking exams, eating in public)

- Excessive fear of AND anxiety reaction to social situations that may cause humiliation, embarrassment, disapproval, disgrace (you'll look stupid, incompetent, weak, panicky, etc.).

- Must cause significant distress or disruption to your normal routine.

OBSESSIVE-COMPULSIVE (2%)

FEAR OF YOUR OWN THOUGHTS, IDEAS, IMAGES, OR IMPULSES
(e.g., contamination, doing something violent to somebody, hitting someone with car, leaving door unlocked, leaving stove on)

- Obsessions - chronic thoughts, ideas, images, or impulses which are intrusive, unwarranted, and unwanted. People are aware that these are a function of their own mind.

- Compulsions - repetitive, ritualized behaviors that one feels driven to perform in order to prevent or neutralize the obsession and reduce their anxiety. (e.g., checking and cleaning rituals, counting, repeating certain words, arranging, etc.).

STEP 2

CHOOSE A TARGET FOR EXPOSURE

Depending on the type of anxiety problem, the target for exposure will differ. It's important to choose the right type of target to maximize the potency of desensitization. For some types of anxiety problems, there is a primary target type and a secondary target type.

- **FOR SPECIFIC PHOBIA**:

    The primary target is the _feared object_ (e.g., dogs) or _circumstance_ (e.g., elevators, flying). So during the initial exposure, the client would be remembering, or visualizing, or re-experiencing the feared object or circumstance in the first person.

- **FOR GENERALIZED ANXIETY**:

    The primary target is the _actual worried thoughts and mental pictures_ and their expected negative outcomes. So during the initial exposure, the client would be visualizing their worried mental pictures and thinking the worried thoughts as they typically would have done in various anxious situations.

- **FOR PANIC:**

  Many times the "trigger" for a panic attack is a specific body sensation that is experienced during heightened anxiety (e.g., dizziness, chest pain, hard to breathe, etc.). The person's reaction to these body sensations may then bring on a full panic attack because they are interpreted as highly dangerous (e.g., suffocating, having a heart attack) or highly embarrassing in public. Therefore, the primary target for exposure is the *specific body sensation*. Following that, the types of situations that the person is afraid they might have a panic attack in can be used as a secondary target. So during the initial exposure, the client would be re-experiencing at least one primary body sensation that occurs during panic attacks. One way to get the client to re-experience the sensation(s) is to have them remember a past panic attack situation. If this is not enough to elicit the physical sensation(s), then:

  ⇨ USE THE "TECHNIQUES FOR ELICITING A SPECIFIC BODY SENSATION AS A TARGET" (p. 39)

- **FOR POST-TRAUMATIC STRESS:**

  The primary target is the *original memory*. Following that, one or more current triggers (e.g., loud noises, people that look like the abuser) can be used as secondary targets. So during the initial exposure, the client would be remembering, or visualizing, or retelling out loud what occurred during the original memory in the first person.

- **FOR SOCIAL ANXIETY:**

  The primary target is one or more kinds of *social situations*. So during the initial exposure, the client would be remembering, or visualizing, or re-experiencing what occurred during a specific social situation in first person.

- **FOR OBSESSIVE-COMPULSIVE DISORDER:**

  The primary target is the *obsessive thoughts and images* (e.g., getting contaminated, forgetting to lock a door, fear of harming her child) that then lead to performing compulsions or rituals (e.g., excessive hand washing, checking/rechecking, repeating a prayer to oneself) that serve to neutralize the distress associated with thoughts. So during the initial exposure, the client would be thinking their obsessive thoughts and visualizing their mental pictures. The key in OCD is to help clients learn that they can control their anxiety while having obsessive thoughts WITHOUT RESORTING TO DOING COMPULSIONS.

STEP 3

IDENTIFY THE IRRATIONAL, CATASTROPHIC, DISTORTED THOUGHTS, PICTURES, BELIEFS, ASSUMPTIONS, & EXPECTATIONS

1. Across different anxiety problems, anxious cognitions tend to:

    - Over-estimate the likelihood of occurrence of negative events (predictions as facts).

    - Over-estimate the risk of danger in terms of the client's safety and unpredictability.

    - Under-estimate the client's own ability to cope and control the situation.

    - Affirm the belief that when bad things do happen, it will be intolerable and unbearable.

    - Affirm the belief that worry shifting (not allowing oneself to experience the worried thoughts to their conclusion), avoiding situations, and self-distracting are helpful strategies with anxiety.

2. Different types of anxiety problems are typically associated with different types of anxious cognitions. Below are examples of anxious cognitions by type of anxiety problem.

    - **SPECIFIC PHOBIA**

        Airplanes seem to be crashing all the time these days.
        I don't know how elevators stay up.
        I'll suffocate in the elevator.
        I can't handle scary situations.
        I won't be able to handle the needle.
        The bridge could fall in while I'm on it.

Dogs attack me because they see I'm afraid.
I'll go crazy from the anxiety.
No one else has this problem as bad as me.
I'm so weak.
I can't stand it.

- **GENERALIZED ANXIETY**

    I'm inadequate.
    I'm responsible for everything.
    I'm going to fail.
    Something terrible is going to happen.
    I'm never good enough.
    I can't handle anything.
    If people knew what I was really like, they'd reject me.
    Anxiety is a sign of weakness.
    I'm a failure.
    Things will never turn out well.
    I won't be able to fix it.
    I'll be left all alone.
    I'll be poor and living on the street.
    What if it's cancer, M.S., etc?
    What if the business never makes it?
    Nothing is working out.
    I don't have anything going for me.
    I won't be able to handle it if it doesn't work out.

- **PANIC**

    I'll have a panic attack.
    I won't be able to get out of here.
    My heart will start racing.
    I'll pass out.
    I'll have an asthma attack.
    I'm having a heart attack.
    I'll vomit.
    I won't be able to breathe.
    I'm going to die.

I'll embarrass myself.
I won't be able to get help.
I'll lose control.
People will think I'm crazy.
People will see me and laugh.
I must have a brain tumor.

- **POST-TRAUMATIC STRESS**

    What happened is my fault.
    I should have been able to prevent it.
    Something terrible could happen at anytime.
    I'm in danger now.
    I can't let my guard down.
    I'm helpless.
    You can't trust anyone.
    No one will be there to help me if I need it.
    There's no point in trying to control anything.
    I have to be on alert at all times.
    It's better to avoid potentially dangerous situations.
    The world is unpredictable and dangerous.
    I'm powerless to prevent a catastrophe.
    Life is meaningless.
    I won't be able to stand another loss.
    If I get too close to someone, they'll leave or die.
    Why is the world so cruel?

- **SOCIAL ANXIETY**

    I'll look like an idiot.
    They'll see I don't have anything intelligent to say.
    I'll say something stupid.
    I'll freeze up.
    I'm boring.
    They can see how nervous I am.
    Everybody is looking at me.
    They're all better, smarter, funnier, etc. than me.
    They think I'm a fool.

That was terrible.
No one liked me.
They're trying to exclude me and I probably deserve it.
I blew it again.
He doesn't like me...so there's probably something really wrong with me.
If I disagree, they'll get mad at me.
I can't show how weak I really am.
I have to make a good impression.
I have to get their approval.
I'm odd.
I don't have what it takes to be successful.
I'm different from everyone else.
Why would they want to listen to me?
I won't have the answers.
They won't believe me.
They'll think "what's wrong with this guy"?

- **OBSESSIVE-COMPULSIVE**

  There are germs everywhere.
  I've been contaminated.
  I have to clean this right now or I'll go crazy.
  I could do or say something unacceptable without realizing it.
  If I don't wash my hands, I could spread germs to my whole family.
  What if I forgot to lock the door? I have to be sure. I'd better check.
  I'll feel better if I do *x* again.
  Better safe than sorry.
  I'm a terrible person for having such thoughts.
  That horrible thought'll come true unless I do something to stop it right now.
  It has to be perfect.
  Thoughts are powerful and can cause bad things to happen.
  If I can't control my thoughts, I won't be able to control my actions.
  I'm to blame if I don't take all possible precautions.
  I'm the only one I can truly count on.

3. Ultimately, the most critical irrational, catastrophic, distorted thoughts, pictures, beliefs, assumptions, and expectations are unique and idiosyncratic to each client. Identifying these client-specific cognitions takes more time than presuming they are generic or general across clients with a particular type of anxiety. The worksheets below can help facilitate this process with the client.

⇨ USE THE "ANXIETY REACTION AND TRAUMA REACTION" WORKSHEETS (p. 41)

STEP 4

DEVELOP BEHAVIORAL SKILLS FOR RELAXING PHYSICALLY AND MENTALLY

A high physiologic level of anxiety itself is a contributing factor to one's inability to think clearly, handle, and cope successfully with challenging situations. It's important, therefore, to be able to teach a client skills at remaining calmer and more relaxed in order to counter and interrupt high levels of physical and physiologic anxiety. Six behavioral skills for relaxing physically and mentally are described below. The three most primary skills are: (1) muscle relaxation (either progressive or passive or both), (2) abdominal breathing, and (3) visualization (either forest, beach, or special place). The Container and Eye movement skills are usually secondary skills to teach, when needed.

1. **TEACH THE CLIENT PROGRESSIVE MUSCLE RELAXATION**

    Progressive muscle relaxation involves actively tensing, and then subsequently relaxing, different muscle groups of your body. The idea is akin to stretching a rubber band, and then releasing it, in that a person can: (1) better experience the difference between the tense and the relaxed state, and (2) can better maximize the relaxed state because it allows a "letting go" from the tense state.

    ⇨ USE THE "PROGRESSIVE MUSCLE RELAXATION" SCRIPTS #1 and #2 (p. 43)

2. **TEACH THE CLIENT PASSIVE MUSCLE RELAXATION**

   Passive muscle relaxation involves relaxing different parts of your body by mentally "telling yourself" or cueing yourself ("relax", "let go") to relax. Unlike progressive relaxation, you do not actively move or tense your muscles.

   ⇨ USE THE "PASSIVE MUSCLE RELAXATION" SCRIPTS #1 AND #2 (p. 52)

3. **TEACH THE CLIENT ABDOMINAL, SLOW, DEEP BREATHING**

   Changes in breathing are a significant factor in heightened anxiety levels, especially in the case of panic episodes. Breathing is often shallow (from the chest) and fast. Also, hyperventilation (overbreathing) or breath holding may be occurring, where oxygen levels are out of balance relative to carbon dioxide levels. Therefore, it's very important to teach clients several aspects of good breathing including: (1) slowing down the breathing to about 10 breaths per minute, and (2) breathing more deeply and from the abdomen.

   ⇨ USE THE "BREATHING TECHNIQUES" SCRIPTS (p. 56)

4. **CREATE A SPECIAL, CALM, PEACEFUL, SAFE PLACE**

   Identify and practice experiencing a "place" which you would associate with calmness, peacefulness, and safety. This place can be real, imaginary, or symbolic, and may include nurturing and protective people, natural and man-made objects, animals, sounds, voices, smells, etc.

   ⇨ USE THE "CREATING A SPECIAL PLACE" SCRIPT (p. 59)

   ⇨ USE THE "BEACH AND FOREST SPECIAL PLACES" SCRIPTS (p. 61)

5. **CREATE A "CONTAINER" FOR ANXIOUS THOUGHTS AND IMAGES**

Suppressing and interrupting anxious thinking and mental pictures can be a helpful short-term technique for reducing anxiety levels and allowing the person more time to apply longer-term coping skills. This technique involves first identifying and then using a "symbolic container" (e.g., box, safe, behind a wall or protective shield, a shelf, etc.) or some distancing device (put on a ship, plane, balloon, etc.) in order to safely "contain", "put away", or "send away" the anxious thoughts and images. Practice by having the client choose something **mildly to moderately** anxiety producing and then containing, putting it away, or sending it away. Then repeat the process several times.

6. **USE THE EYE-MOVEMENT TECHNIQUE**

Suppressing and interrupting anxious thinking and mental pictures can be a helpful short-term technique for reducing anxiety levels and allowing the person more time to apply longer-term coping skills. This technique involves having clients relatively quickly move their eyes from side to side at the rate of about two back-and-forth movements per second. About 20-30 back-and-forth sets are standard. This process appears to suppress or disrupt anxious thoughts and images. Practice by having the client choose something **mildly to moderately** anxiety producing. Then have them follow your finger (held about 12-14" from their face) with their head held still, while you move your finger back-and-forth across the client's line of vision. Next, the client should practice moving their eyes back-and-forth on their own using the corners of the room or their knees to focus on. Clients can do the self eye-movements with their eyes closed as well.

STEP 5

DEVELOP NEW COGNITIVE RESOURCES AND COPING SKILLS

One of the most important components of the exposure process is developing counter and coping - thoughts, expectations, assumptions, beliefs, and mental pictures - which are more calm, positive, resourceful, realistic, confident, and coping. Given that everyone's thoughts and mental pictures are different, it's important to develop highly individualized counter statements and pictures. In order to initially "loosen" a client's conviction to their anxious thoughts and images, it is helpful to have them evaluate what they say and picture to themselves in anxious situations. The worksheet referenced below can facilitate this process with a client.

⇨ USE THE "16 THINGS TO ASK YOURSELF ABOUT YOUR THOUGHTS, BELIEFS, ASSUMPTIONS, AND EXPECTATIONS" QUESTIONS (p. 63)

You can use FOUR DIFFERENT METHODS to help the client develop new counter and coping thoughts, self-talk, and mental pictures. They are:

Past Experience   Remember, think of, or find a time in the past, in a similar kind of situation, when you were able to handle things more like you want to now...even if you were only able to accomplish some of what you're wanting to now. Remember that now and put yourself back into that situation now. What were you able to say to yourself, believe, remind yourself, picture to yourself, feel emotionally, and do back then that would help you now?.

Future Projection   Imagine it's some time (____ months/years) in the future when you have already figured out how to handle this kind of situation. Put yourself into the future. What are you able to say to yourself, believe, remind yourself, picture to yourself, feel emotionally, and do in this future time that would help you in the present?

Magic Wand   Imagine you had a magic wand and you could use it to (or are magically given the ability to) handle this situation that way you want to. What would it give you the ability to say to yourself, believe, remind yourself, picture to yourself, feel emotionally, and do in this kind of situation?

Model or Coach   Think about someone else - real or fictional, public or you know personally, living or passed away - who knows how to handle this kind of situation the way you wish you could. What would they coach you to say to yourself, believe, remind yourself, picture to yourself, feel emotionally, and do in this kind of situation? What would they be able to do on the inside or outside that you could try out for yourself.

There are a number of things to consider when helping clients develop well designed and potent counter and coping self-statements and pictures. They are:

1. Well designed counter and coping self-statements and pictures modify basic assumptions made in anxious situations to be more realistic, more positive, and more resourceful in the following ways:

    - More realistic estimate of the likelihood of occurrence of a negative outcome.

    - More realistic estimate of the risk of danger in terms of the client's safety and predictability.

    - More realistic estimate of the client's own ability to cope and control the situation.

    - More resourceful and positive beliefs and expectations that when bad things do happen, the client will be able to tolerate and cope with it.

    - More resourceful and positive beliefs and expectations that worry shifting, avoiding feared circumstances, and distracting themselves will not help them and will only reinforce their anxiety.

2. Some common counter and coping self-talk used in different phases of anxious situations are listed below. However, remember that these only provide a general guideline.

    PREPARING EARLY BEFORE THINGS GET ANXIOUS

    Worrying won't make it go better.
    What exactly do I have to do?
    Just think rationally. My negative thoughts aren't very rational.
    I can plan how to deal with this before it happens.
    I know I'll get better with practice.
    I'm going to get through this.
    It's easier once I get started and jump in.
    Tomorrow I'll be through it.
    This is going to upset me, but I can deal with it.
    What is it that I have to do?
    I can work out a plan to handle this.
    Try not to take this too seriously.
    This could be a nasty situation, but I have to believe in myself.

COPING WITH THE SITUATION WITHOUT BEING OVERWHELMED

I need to take it one step at a time and go slow.
Remember to breathe.
I can ride this through.
This is just a false alarm... an over-reaction of my body.
I need to let this anxiety rise and fall and pass.
This isn't dangerous, it's just anxiety.
I can do this... I'm doing it now.
The tension I feel is a signal to relax and think differently.
I can get help if I need it.
When I don't scare myself, I can handle this more easily.
I don't have to like this, I just have to get through it.
I'm safe right now.
It's just a memory.
If other people can do this, so can I.
This will be over soon, nothing lasts forever.
I'm only this afraid because I decided to be.
I'll get used to this with practice.
I've survived this kind of thing before.
I can keep this within limits that I can handle.
Focus on the next step.
Fear is natural, it goes up and down in intensity.
There are worse things.
I need to keep my mind off this and on what I have to do to handle it.
I have to continue to relax and stay calm.
Just get a grip on yourself. You can handle this.

GIVING MYSELF CREDIT AFTERWARDS

I'm getting better with each try.
I can actually change this.
I did it.
It wasn't as bad as I imagined.
My thoughts about it are worse than the thing itself.
Next time, it won't feel as intense.
I'm able to actually relax with the anxiety.
I should tell ___ about this.

3. Well designed mental images, pictures, and movies facilitate the client seeing and picturing:

 - Themselves, in the first person, tolerating, handling, and coping with the situation better (e.g., handling the social conversation) because they have stayed calmer and were thinking about the situation differently.

 - A more successful and positive outcome to an anxious situation (e.g. plane lands safely at the destination).

 - Themselves, in the first person, handling the situation the way they would like to (e.g., handling the rejection) as you feel more capable now (although you don't have to like it).

 - Themselves, in the first person, being able to accomplish various things because they are gaining freedom from the anxiety and its restrictions (e.g. being able to take the trip).

 - One or more of their own past successes in any challenging situation rather than focusing on negative memories or negative predicted outcomes.

 - A model, coach, nurturer, or supporter who can handle the situation the way they want to want to and/or who is guiding and comforting them through this.

 - Their "child" part of self as being the one who is actually afraid and picturing protecting or comforting that "child".

4. The worksheet referenced below can be used to help the client remember and document their new self-statements and mental pictures you develop with them.

 ⇨ USE THE "POSITIVE COUNTER-STATEMENTS AND PICTURES" WORKSHEET (p. 65)

STEP 6

DEVELOP A GRADED HIERARCHY

A graded hierarchy serves to break the anxious target into smaller pieces from least to most anxiety provoking or anxiety arousing. The client is then exposed to a lower level item and works their way up to the most anxiety provoking items. The hierarchy for the same type of anxiety problem will be different for different people because of what arouses that person's anxiety and at what level of arousal. Graded hierarchies typically have between eight and twenty steps.

AN EXAMPLE GRADED HIERARCHY FOR **SOCIAL ANXIETY** MIGHT BE:

- E-mailing a family member
- Talking to family member at a birthday party
- Talking to a male co-worker before a group meeting
- Talking to a female co-worker by dropping by her desk
- Talking to relative stranger who's part of a group getting together after work
- Talking to a male stranger at a party
- Talking to a female stranger at a party
- Going on a blind date.

AN EXAMPLE HIERARCHY FOR A **SPECIFIC PHOBIA OF FLYING** MIGHT BE:

- Packing luggage
- Making reservations
- Driving to the airport
- Checking in
- See the planes at the airport
- Boarding the plane
- Taxiing
- Moving around the cabin
- Climbing to cruising altitude
- Descending
- Waiting for departure

AN EXAMPLE GRADED HIERARCHY FOR A **SPECIFIC PHOBIA OF ELEVATORS** MIGHT BE:

> ☞ Standing outside an elevator and not getting in
> Standing outside an elevator and thinking of getting in
> Getting in the elevator with the door keep open
> Being in the elevator with a friend and the doors closed
> Going up/down one floor on the elevator with a friend
> Going up/down many floors with a friend
> Being in the elevator alone
> Going up/down one floor alone
> Going up/down many floors alone

AN EXAMPLE GRADED HIERARCHY FOR **GENERALIZED ANXIETY ABOUT A FAMILY MEMBER** MIGHT BE:

> ☞ Worried that my daughter will be demeaned by a family member
> Worried that my daughter will be demeaned by me because I got so frustrated
> Worried that my daughter will get temporarily lost in a crowd
> Worried that my daughter will be hurt by someone who breaks into the house in the daytime without a weapon
> Worried that the economy will get so bad that I'll loose my job and won't be able to take care of my daughter
> Worried that my daughter will be hurt by someone who breaks into the house at night with a weapon
> Worried that my daughter will be abducted by a stranger

⇨ USE THE "GRADED HIERARCHY" WORKSHEET (p. 66)

STEP 7

LEARN THE SUDs SCALE TO KEEP TRACK OF THE LEVEL OF ANXIETY
("3" as normal tension)

The SUDs scale provides a relatively simple way to measure a client's level of anxiety on a scale from 0-10. The numbers represent the following:

- **0**   **Complete Relaxation**. No distress at all. Deep asleep.

- **1**   **Very Relaxed**. Awake but dosing off.

- **2**   **Relaxing** at the beach, relaxing at home in front of a warm fire on a wintry day, walking peacefully in the woods. Your mind wanders some.

- **3**   **The Amount of Tension Needed To Keep One's Attention** from wandering, to keep one's head erect, etc. the tension is not experienced as unpleasant in any way.

- **4**   **Mild Distress**. Mild feelings of bodily tension, mild worry, mild apprehension, mild fear or anxiety). Somewhat unpleasant but easily tolerated.

- **5**   **Mild to Moderate Distress**. Unpleasant, mild bodily symptoms.

- **6**   **Moderate Distress**, but still able to work, drive a car, etc. distinctly unpleasant feelings of fear/anxiety, anger, worry, apprehension, substantial bodily tension, headache, stomach upset but tolerable sensations and distress. A "bad day."

- **7**   **Moderately High Distress**. Hard to concentrate.

- **8**   **High Distress**. High levels of fear, anxiety, worry, apprehension, bodily tension. Thinking is impaired.

- **9**   **High to Extreme Distress**. Bodily distress high, thinking impaired, problem solving is poor.

- **10**   **Extreme Distress**. Panic stricken, terror stricken, extreme bodily tension. The maximum amount of fear, anxiety, or apprehension you can possibly imagine. Thinking, work, and social relations are all substantially impaired.

STEP 8

OPTIONAL RELAXATION EXERCISE

Do any of the relaxation exercises for about 10-15 minutes. Have the client tell you their SUDs level until the SUDs level is 3 or lower.

STEP 9

START IMAGINAL EXPOSURE

Exposure trials start with the LEAST anxiety-provoking items/steps on the guided exposure hierarchy and then progress to the MOST anxiety-provoking items/steps. If some items provoke only minimal anxiety, choose something on the guided hierarchy that provokes at least a 4 SUDs level but won't elicit more than an 8 level. Each exposure trial should continue ideally until the SUDs rating has dropped by at least half. It's important that exposure not be terminated before the client has experienced some decrease in anxiety, otherwise the association between the feared stimulus and anxiety reaction will be maintained or even strengthen. The length of an exposure trial will vary, from 5 minutes to as long as 45 minutes, depending on the step in the hierarchy and the ability of the client to reduce their anxiety to the feared stimulus. Repeat the exposure for the same item/step up to 5 times each. It's often better to do fewer trials of greater length than to do many short exposures. Each imaginal exposure trial is comprised of phase 1 and phase 2 below.

PHASE 1 OF THE IMAGINAL EXPOSURE TRIAL:

In Imagination, Have The Client <u>Begin to Expose Themselves</u> To The Feared Memory, Body Sensations, Object, Circumstance, Social Situation, Worried Thoughts And Pictures, Obsessive Thoughts, Etc.

- <u>The Client Needs to Challenge Themselves but Not Overwhelm Themselves</u>. (Say: "you need to face the fear to conquer it", "you're in complete control of this now", "you need to stay with this to overcome it", "the anxiety level will go down in time").

- The Client Needs to Experience the Anxiety Fully Before Using Countering And Coping Skills (At Least 4+ SUDs). This Allows Them to <u>Stay with it Long Enough to Experience And Evaluate</u> the Specific Details, Internal Dialogue, Beliefs, Expectations, Mental Pictures, Etc.

PHASE 2 OF THE IMAGINAL EXPOSURE TRIAL:

Have The Client <u>Begin To Counter And Cope</u> Until The SUDs Level Decreases By ½ At Each Trial. Use:

- Counter/Coping Self-Talk
- Counter/Coping Mental Pictures
- Passive Muscle Relaxation
- Abdominal, Slow, Deep Breathing
- Container Technique (optional)
- Eye-Movement Technique (optional)

Don't allow the client to worry shift, mentally distract, escape, avoid, or apply safety tactics. The goal here is to stay in contact with, confront, and manage the anxious target. Ask the client to report their SUDs level regularly. Repeat multiple trials until the target can only produce a 3-4 SUDs level.

IF THE SUDs LEVEL GETS TOO HIGH (8-10 OR ABOVE), USE ONE OF TECHNIQUES BELOW DURING EXPOSURE

- Use the Eye Movement Technique to Distract and Interrupt.
- Freeze the Image.
- Change the Movie to a Still Photo.
- Turn the Image into Black & White.
- Watch it in the 3rd Person like Watching a Movie/video or as Though it was Happening to Someone Else.
- Watch the Image While Hovering Far Above It.
- Place a Protective Shield or Glass Wall Around You.
- Zoom the Image Out or Shrink it to the Size of a Postage Stamp.

IF HIGH ANXIETY PERSISTS, OR
IT'S DIFFICULT TO MOVE PAST A PARTICULAR STEP:

- Break Down that Step of the Hierarchy into Several Smaller Steps.

- Add an Intermediate Step to the Hierarchy.

- Return to an Earlier (Lower) Step in the Hierarchy.

STEP 10

IN-VIVO EXPOSURE

In-vivo exposure involves exposing the client to the real-life situation, object, or event (e.g., going to the party, using the elevator, being in the situation where you might have a panic attack, etc.) rather than experiencing it in one's imagination. In in-vivo exposure, phase 1 would be replaced by being in the real life situation and phase 2 would remain the same. In-vivo exposure has been shown to be an extremely powerful and effective form of exposure therapy for anxiety problems, particularly where the feared stimulus is more external (specific phobias, panic sensations) rather than more internal (generalized anxiety, OCD). PTSD and social anxiety have aspects of both external (e.g., trauma triggers, dealing with judgmental people) and internal (e.g., the memory of the trauma, believing you're inadequate socially) feared stimuli.

SECTION 3:

CLINICAL TOOLS

Clyde M. Feldman, Ph.D.

ANXIETY INVENTORY

1. Do you have spontaneous panic attacks that come out of the blue?   Yes ___ No ___

2. Have you had at least four such attacks in the last month?   Yes ___ No ___

3. In your worst experience with panic, did you have four or more of the following symptoms?   Yes ___ No ___

    ☐ shortness of breath or smothering sensation
    ☐ dizziness or unsteady feeling
    ☐ heart palpitations or rapid heartbeat
    ☐ trembling or shaking
    ☐ sweating
    ☐ choking
    ☐ nausea or abdominal distress
    ☐ feelings of being detached or out of touch with your body
    ☐ numbness or tingling sensations
    ☐ flushes or chills
    ☐ chest pain or discomfort
    ☐ fear of dying
    ☐ fear of going crazy or doing something out of control

4. Does fear of having panic attacks cause you to avoid going into certain situations? Yes ___ No ___

5. Which of the following situations do you avoid because you are afraid of panicking?

    ☐ going far away from home
    ☐ shopping in a grocery store
    ☐ standing in a grocery store line
    ☐ going to department stores
    ☐ going to shopping malls
    ☐ driving on freeways
    ☐ driving on surface streets far from home

- ☐ driving anywhere by yourself
- ☐ using public transportation (buses, trains, etc.)
- ☐ going over bridges (whether you're the driver or passenger)
- ☐ going through tunnels (as driver or passenger)
- ☐ flying in planes
- ☐ riding in elevators
- ☐ being in high places
- ☐ going to a dentist's or doctor's office
- ☐ sitting in a barber's or beautician's chair
- ☐ eating in restaurants
- ☐ going to work
- ☐ being too far from a safe person or safe place
- ☐ being alone
- ☐ going outside your house
- ☐ other _____

6. Do you avoid certain situations, not primarily because you are afraid of panicking, but because you're afraid of feeling social embarrassment or being negatively evaluated by other people?   Yes ___ No ___

7. Which of the following situations do you avoid because of a fear of social embarrassment or being negatively evaluated by other people?

   - ☐ sitting in any kind of group (at work, in school classrooms, social organizations, self-help groups, etc.)
   - ☐ giving a talk or presentation before a small group of people
   - ☐ giving a talk or presentation before a large group of people
   - ☐ parties and social functions
   - ☐ using public restrooms
   - ☐ eating in front of others
   - ☐ writing or signing your name in the presence of others
   - ☐ any situation where you might say something foolish
   - ☐ other _____

8. Do you fear and avoid any one (or more than one) of the following? But your avoidance is **NOT** due to a fear of having a panic attack or a fear of feeling social embarrassment.

    ☐ insects or animals (spiders, bees, snakes, rats, bats, dogs, etc.)
    ☐ heights (high floors in buildings, tops of hills or mountains, bridges, etc.)
    ☐ elevators
    ☐ airplanes
    ☐ doctors or dentists
    ☐ thunder or lightning
    ☐ water
    ☐ blood
    ☐ illness such as heart attacks or cancer
    ☐ darkness
    ☐ other _____

9. Do you feel quite anxious a lot of the time but it is **NOT** because of fear of panic attacks or because of phobias, or social embarrassment?   Yes ___ No ___

10. Have you been very worried for at least six months about two or more problems in your life such as finances, health, relationships, family, or school?   Yes ___ No ___

11. Do you have at least six of the following symptoms because you're anxious and worried about the kinds of things in question 10?   Yes ___ No ___

    ☐ trembling or feeling shaky
    ☐ muscle tension
    ☐ restlessness
    ☐ weariness or fatigue
    ☐ shortness of breath
    ☐ heart palpitations or racing heart
    ☐ sweating
    ☐ dry mouth
    ☐ abdominal distress or nausea
    ☐ lightheadedness or dizziness
    ☐ hot flashes or chills

- ☐ frequent urination
- ☐ lump in threat
- ☐ a feeling of being keyed up or on edge
- ☐ jumpiness or being easily startled
- ☐ difficulty concentrating or your mind goes blank
- ☐ trouble falling asleep or staying asleep
- ☐ irritability

12. Do any of the unpleasant thoughts listed below seem to enter your mind without you wanting them to. And although you know that they're irrational, you have a hard time keeping them from repeatedly coming into your mind?   Yes ___ No ___

    - ☐ thoughts of being contaminated by dirt, germs, chemicals, or other substances
    - ☐ thoughts of death or terrible things happening like fire, burglary, flooding, etc.
    - ☐ thoughts of harm coming to a loved one because you weren't careful enough
    - ☐ thoughts of you physically harming a loved one, poisoning someone, hitting a pedestrian with your car, pushing someone in front a moving vehicle, etc.
    - ☐ thoughts of losing something valuable
    - ☐ thoughts of a sexual or religious nature that normally are very unacceptable to you

13. Do you feel driven to do any of the behaviors listed below repeatedly or excessively? These behaviors often help relieve your anxieties about the thoughts in question 12.   Yes ___ No ___

    - ☐ washing your hands, washing parts of your body, or grooming
    - ☐ cleaning things
    - ☐ checking lights, water faucets, the stove, door locks, or the emergency brake
    - ☐ counting to yourself or repeating words or phrases to yourself
    - ☐ touching objects or people in a certain way or a certain number of times
    - ☐ arranging objects in a certain way or keeping things in a certain order
    - ☐ doing certain actions a specific number of times or in a very specific way like when you go through a doorway or getting in/out of a chair, etc.
    - ☐ avoiding certain colors, certain numbers, or certain names that you associate with unpleasant thoughts or events
    - ☐ confessing that you said or did something incorrectly or wrong

14. Were you ever in a traumatic situation that made you feel intense fear, terror, or helpless - like being physically or sexually abused as a child, being the victim of domestic violence as an adult, being assaulted or raped, being present during a violent crime, being in a particularly bad car /plane/train accident, or being in a natural disaster?   Yes ___ No ___

15. If you said yes above, do you have any of the following symptoms which have lasted for at least one month or longer?

    ☐ repetitive, distressing thoughts about the situation
    ☐ nightmares related to the situation
    ☐ flashbacks so intense that you feel or act as though the traumatic situation were occurring all over again
    ☐ an attempt to avoid thoughts or feelings associated with the traumatic situation
    ☐ an attempt to avoid activities or places associated with the traumatic situation (like a phobia about driving after you've been an car accident)
    ☐ emotional numbness -or being out of touch with your feelings
    ☐ feeling detached or distant from others
    ☐ a loss of interest in activities that used to give you pleasure
    ☐ anxiety symptoms, such as difficultly falling asleep or staying asleep, difficulty concentrating, being startled easily, or having a lot of irritability and outbursts of anger

ANXIETY INVENTORY SCORING

QUESTIONS 1, 2 3, 4 AND 5: PANIC DISORDER (with or w/o Agoraphobia)

If the answers to Q1 and Q2 were YES, it's likely you have PANIC.

If the answer to Q1 was Yes, but you had fewer than four attacks and/or fewer than four of the symptoms listed, than you likely DO NOT have full-blown panic disorder but rather LIMITED SYMPTOM ATTACKS.

If the answer to Q4 was YES, you may have Panic WITH AGORAPHOBIA. The number of situations checked in Q5 indicates the extent of the Agoraphobia and the degree to which it limits your activities.

QUESTIONS 6 AND 7: SOCIAL ANXIETY DISORDER

If the answer to Q6 was YES, it's likely you have SOCIAL ANXIETY. The number of situations checked in Q7 indicates the degree of the Social Anxiety problem.

QUESTION 8: SPECIFIC PHOBIA DISORDER

If one or more items in Q8 was checked, it's likely you have one or more SPECIFIC PHOBIAS.

QUESTIONS 9, 10, AND 11: GENERALIZED ANXIETY DISORDER

If the answers to Q9, Q10, and Q11 were YES, it's likely that you have GENERALIZED ANXIETY.

If the answer to Q9 was yes, but Q10 and/or Q1I were not, you likely have an anxiety condition that is not severe enough to be Generalized Anxiety.

QUESTIONS 12 AND 13: OBSESSIVE-COMPULSIVE DISORDER

If the answers to Q12 and Q13 were YES, it's likely that you have OBSESSIVE-COMPULSION.

If the answer to Q12 was yes, but Q13 was no, it's likely that you have Obsessive - Compulsion but have obsessions only.

QUESTIONS 14 AND 15: POST-TRAUMATIC STRESS DISORDER

If the answers to Q14 and Q15 were YES, it's likely that you have POST-TRAUMATIC STRESS.

IDENTIFYING CURRENT TRIGGERS

LIST EACH OF THE TRIGGERS THAT YOU HAVE AN OVERLY STRONG NEGATIVE EMOTIONAL REACTION TO (e.g., anxious, afraid, worried, humiliated, etc.). A TRIGGER CAN BE WHAT SOMEONE DOES OR SAYS, HOW SOMEONE ACTS, A TYPE OF SITUATION, A PLACE, CERTAIN OBJECTS, CERTAIN SOUNDS OR SMELLS, OR SOMETHING YOU SEE ON T.V. OR READ ABOUT. AFTER YOU LIST THE TRIGGERS, RATE EACH TRIGGER'S STRENGTH, INTENSITY, OR POWER FROM 1 (lowest) TO 10 (highest).

1. _____

2. _____

3. _____

4. _____

5. _____

6. _____

7. _____

8. _____

TECHNIQUES FOR ELICITING A SPECIFIC BODY SENSATION AS A TARGET

USE ONE OR MORE OF THE TECHNIQUES BELOW TO:

1. Help Identify What Specific Body Sensation(s) Is Associated with Increased Anxiety and Thereby a Trigger for a Panic Attack.

2. Help the Client Practice Re-experiencing the Body Sensation(s) So That it Can Be Used as a Target in the Exposure Process.

HEAD SHAKING: Shake your head loosely from side to side for 30 seconds to produce dizziness or disorientation.

HEAD LIFTING: Place your head between your legs for 30 seconds and then lift it quickly to produce lightheadedness or the sensation of blood rushing from your head.

STEPPING UP/RUNNING IN PLACE: Take one step up, using stairs, a box, or a footstool, and immediately step down. Repeat the stepping for 1 minute and at a fast enough rate to notice your heart pumping quickly, to produce racing heart and shortness of breath. Alternatively, you many run or jog in place.

BREATH HOLDING: Hold your breath for as long as you can or for about 30 seconds to produce chest tightness and smothering sensations.

BODY TENSING: Tense every part of your body (e.g., arms, legs, stomach, back, shoulder, face, etc.) without causing pain, for 1 minute, to produce muscle tension, weakness, and trembling. Alternatively, try holding a push-up position for 1 minute or for as long as you can.

SPINNING: Spin around and around for 1 minute to produce dizziness. A chair that swivels, such as a desk chair, is ideal for this exercise, and is even better if someone can spin you around. Alternatively, stand up and turn around quickly several times, but have a soft chair or couch nearby to sit on afterwards. Note that this exercise many cause nausea as well. Those who suffer from motion sickness (i.e., vomit after amusement-park rides or in back seat on winding roads, etc.) may become very nauseated and even vomit after this exercise. Anyone who suffers motion sickness should either skip to the other exercises or spin slowly.

HYPERVENTILATING: While standing or sitting, hyperventilate for 1 minute by breathing deeply and quickly and with great force to produce a sense of unreality, shortness of breath, tingling, cold or hot feelings, dizziness or headache, and so forth.

STRAW BREATHING: Breathe through a thin straw for 1 minute without allowing any air through your nose (hold your nostrils together) to produce sensations of restricted airflow or smothering. Alternatively, breathe as slowly as possible for 1 minute.

STARING: Stare as intensely as possible at a small spot on the wall or at your refection in the mirror for 2 minutes to produce sensations of unreality.

ANXIETY REACTION WORKSHEET

SITUATION: Describe the situation. It may be one where you were by yourself or with others.

_____

_____

_____

PHYSICAL & EMOTIONAL REACTIONS: List as many as you had in the situation.

_____

_____

_____

AUTOMATIC THOUGHTS: Write down the negative thoughts, beliefs, assumptions, expectations, and mental pictures that were going through your mind about yourself, other people, the situation, the future, etc. Also rate your belief in each of these from 1% (not really) to 100% (completely)

_____

_____

_____

LEVEL OF ANXIETY: Rate the intensity from 1-10 (high) _____

OUTCOME: What was the actual outcome or result of the situation which may have been very different than your worst fear or worry.

_____

_____

Clyde M. Feldman, Ph.D.

TRAUMA REACTION WORKSHEET

SITUATION & TRIGGERS: Describe the situation, especially the triggers like physical surroundings, sights, sounds, smells, things done or said, etc.

_____

_____

_____

MEMORIES & SENSATIONS: List the negative, uncomfortable, or distressing memories or sensation that this situation triggered.

_____

_____

_____

AUTOMATIC THOUGHTS: Write down the negative thoughts, beliefs, assumptions, expectations, and mental pictures that were going through your mind about yourself, other people, the situation, the future, etc. Also rate your belief in each of these from 1% (not really) to 100% (completely).

_____

_____

_____

_____

LEVEL OF ANXIETY: Rate the intensity from 1-10 (high) _____

PROGRESSIVE MUSCLE RELAXATION SCRIPT #1

The tension phase of each muscle group should last about 10 seconds, and the relaxation phase should last about 20 seconds.

1. Get into a comfortable position, close your eyes, and just sit quietly for a few seconds.

2. First, build up the tension in the lower arms by making fists with your hands and pulling your fists up by bending the wrists. Feel the tension through the lower arms, the wrists, the fingers, the knuckles, and the hands. Focus on the tension. Notice the symptoms of pulling, of discomfort, of tightness. Hold the position for 10 seconds. Now, release the tension. Let your hands and lower arms relax onto the chair or bed beside you, with the palms facing down. Focus your attention on the symptoms in your hands and arms. Feel the release from tension. Relax the muscles. Relax for 20 seconds.

3. Now, build up the tension in the upper arms by pulling the arms back and in toward your sides. Try not to tense muscles in other parts of your body, although there will be some overlap. Feel the tension in the back of the arms and radiating up into the shoulders and into the back. Focus on the symptoms of tension. Hold the tension for 10 seconds. Now, release the arms and let them relax heavily down. Focus on your upper arms and feel the difference in the sensations compared to those of tension. Your arms might feel heavy, warm, and relaxed. Relax for 20 seconds.

4. Now, build up the tension in the lower legs by flexing your feet and pulling your toes toward your upper body. Feel the tension as it spreads through your feet, your ankles, your shins, and your calves. Feel the tension spreading down the back of the legs into the feet, under the feet, and around the toes. Focus on those parts of your body. Hold the position for 10 seconds. Now, release the leg tension. Let your legs relax onto the chair or the bed. Feel the difference in the muscles as they relax. Feel the release from tension, the sense of comfort, the warmth, and heaviness of relaxation. Relax for 20 seconds.

5. Now, build up the tension in the upper legs by pulling the knees together and lifting the legs off the bed or chair. Focus on the tightness through the upper legs. Feel the pulling symptoms from the hip down and notice the tension in the legs. Focus on those parts of your body. Hold the position for 10 seconds. Now, release the tension, letting the legs drop heavily down on to the chair or bed. Let the tension disappear. Focus on the feeling of relaxation. Feel the difference in your legs. Focus on the sense of comfort. Relax for 20 seconds.

6. Now, build up the tension in your abdomen by pulling your abdomen in toward the spine, very tightly. Feel the tension. Feel the tightness and focus on that part of your body. Hold the position for 10 seconds. Now, let the abdomen go. Let it go farther and farther. Feel the sense of warmth circulating across your abdomen. Feel the comfort of relaxation. Relax for 20 seconds.

7. Now, build up the tension in your chest by taking in a deep breath and holding it. Your chest is expanded, and the muscles are stretched around your chest. Feel the tension in your front and your back. Hold your breath 10 seconds. Now, slowly let the air escape and resume normal breathing, letting the air flow in and out smoothly and easily. Feel the difference in sensations as the muscles relax, compared to those of tension. Relax for 20 seconds.

8. Now, build up the tension in your shoulders. Imagine your shoulders are on strings and being pulled up toward your ears. Feel the tension around your shoulders, radiating down into your back, up into your neck, and to the back of your head. Focus on those parts of your body. Describe the symptoms to yourself. Hold the position for 10 seconds. Then, let the shoulders droop down. Let them droop farther and farther until they feel very relaxed. Feel the sense of relaxation in that part of your body. Focus on the comfort of relaxation. Relax for 20 seconds.

9. Build up the tension in your neck by pressing the back of your neck toward the chair or bed and pulling your chin down toward your chest. Feel the tightness in the back of the neck and up into the head. Focus on the tension. Hold the position for 10 seconds. Now, release the tension by letting your head rest heavily against the bed or chair. Nothing is holding up your head except the

support behind. Focus on the relaxation and feel the difference in sensations from those of the tension. Relax for 20 seconds.

10. Build up the tension around your mouth, jaw and throat by clenching your teeth and forcing the corners of your mouth back into a forced smile. Hold the tension. Feel the tightness in those parts of your body. Describe the symptoms to yourself. Hold the position for 10 seconds. Now, release the tension by letting the mouth drop down and the muscles around the throat and jaw relax. Focus on the difference in the sensations compared to those of tension. Relax for 20 seconds.

11. Now build up the tension around your eyes by squeezing your eyes tightly together for 10 seconds. Now, release. Let the tension disappear from around your eyes. Feel the difference as the muscles relax. Relax for 20 seconds.

12. Now, build up the tension across the lower forehead by frowning, pulling your eyebrows down and toward the center. Feel the tension across your forehead and the top of your head. Focus on the tension. Hold the position for 10 seconds. Now, release, smoothing out the wrinkles and letting the forehead relax. Feel the difference in the sensations. Relax for 20 seconds.

13. Build up the tension in the upper forehead by raising your eyebrows up as high as possible. Feel the wrinkling and the pulling across the forehead and the top of the head. Hold the tension for 10 seconds. Now, relax, letting the eyebrows rest down and the tension from your forehead leave. Focus on the sensations of relaxation. Feel the difference in sensations compared to those of the tension. Relax for 20 seconds.

14. Now, your whole body is feeling relaxed and comfortable. Counting from one to five, feel yourself becoming even more relaxed. *One*, let all the tension leave your body. *Two*, sinking further and further into relaxation. *Three*, feel more and more relaxed. *Four*, feel very relaxed. *Five*, feel deeply relaxed.

15. As you spend a few minutes in this relaxed state, think about your breathing. Feel the cool air as you breathe in and the warm air as you breathe out. Your breathing is slow and regular. Every time you breathe out, think to yourself the word relax... relax... relax... Feeling comfortable and relaxed. (Continue for l-2 minutes.)

16. Now, counting backward from five to one, gradually feel yourself becoming more alert and awake. *Five*, feel more awake. *Four*, come out of the relaxation. *Three*, feel more alert. *Two*, open your eyes. *One*, sit up.

PROGRESSIVE MUSCLE RELAXATION SCRIPT #2

First, focus all your attention on your right foot. With your right foot flat on the floor, lift your toes upward and fan them outward. This will create tension in your ankle and the calf of your right leg. Hold the tension briefly. Now relax it quickly... just let go completely...

Next, focus on your left foot. Extend your left toes upward and fan them out as far as they will go. Once again, there will be a feeling of tension in your ankle and calf. Hold the tension briefly. Now, relax your left foot completely. When I ask you to release the tension, try to let go as much as possible. The secret in relaxing is in the letting go.

Now tense the muscles in your right thigh by pressing down with your right heel. Press down really hard on the heel of your right foot. Feel the tension. Now relax your heel and thigh-let go and notice the difference. In fact, each time you let go, try to identify the difference in feeling between tension and relaxation. Notice how pleasant it feels just to have your muscles relaxing and letting go.

Let's do the same thing with your right thigh. Tense it as tightly as you can by pressing down with your left heel. Press down hard with your left heel and feel the tension as much as possible. Then let go and relax all over. You may have noticed by now a pleasant sensation as you relax a group of muscles.

Next, direct your attention to your lower back. Arch your back. Arch your back way up and make your back taut and hollow and feel the tension up and down your spine. Hold the tension briefly. Now, relax and sit back comfortably again. As you let go, try to remember that there is no limit to the amount of relaxation you can personally experience. Theoretically, you can relax to the point of infinity. Go ahead and relax your back. Relax your body as much as possible. Just relax further and further, letting the relaxation go deeper and deeper into your muscles.

While you keep the rest of your body relaxed, I want you to clench your right fist Clench your fist tighter and tighter. Study the tension in your hand and arm as you do this. Now relax and let the fingers of your hand become loose, completely loose. Notice how different your arm and your hand feel.

Next, clench your left fist, really tight. Clench it really tight and notice the tension in that arm. Now, let go. Relax your left hand. Let your fingers straighten out and become limp. Notice the difference once again.

Next, bend your right elbow and bring the fingers of your right hand up to your right shoulder. With your fingers touching your shoulder, tense the muscles of your right arm hard. Study that tension in the biceps muscle of your upper arm. All right, now straighten out your arm and let go of the tension. Just relax all your muscles and feel the warm, pleasant heaviness that comes with relaxing completely.

Let's do the same thing with your left arm. Touch your shoulder and tense your left bicep tightly. Hold that tension really tightly and observe it carefully. Now let go, relaxing your left arm. Let it drop limp. Relax it as much as you can. Try to let yourself actually feel the relaxation. Continue to let go. Let your whole body relax further and further into deeper and still deeper levels of relaxation.

Now let's focus on your neck muscles. Press your head back as far as you can. Press it back hard, really hard. Feel the tension in your neck. Hold that tension briefly. Then let go. Let your neck relax as much as possible. Let the muscles loosen so completely that your head is as heavy as a bowling ball. Allow the back of the chair to completely support your head so that your neck muscles can relax totally and completely.

Next, hunch up both of your shoulders. Bring your shoulders right up to your ears, as if you're trying to squeeze your ears with your shoulders. Feel the tension. Hold the tension briefly. Now drop your shoulders, let them go completely limp, and feel the relaxation. Let that relaxation go deeper and deeper into your shoulders. Then let it flow right down into the rest of your body.

Now, raise your eyebrows so that it makes your forehead and the top of your scalp all tight and wrinkly. Feel the tension. Hold the tension briefly. Now, relax your forehead, smooth it out. Try to picture, as in a mirror, your forehead becoming smoother and smoother as the relaxation increases.

Next, squeeze your eyes tightly shut. Tighter and tighter. Feel the tension in your eyelids. Then relax them and keep your eyes closed gently and comfortably. Notice how relaxed your eyes feel.

Finally, let's tense the muscles around your mouth. Clench your jaws and lips. Clench them tightly together and study the tension around your mouth. Then relax those muscles. Let your cheeks and lips hang loose and limp. Relax your jaw and keep your teeth slightly apart as you continue to relax all the muscles around your mouth.

Try to notice the contrast throughout your entire body between tension and relaxation. If any tension has crept back into your body, release it and let it go. In your mind's eye, picture your face as though looking in a mirror and actually see the relaxation all over your face. Observe it all over your forehead. Actually feel the relaxation progress further and further. Just allow yourself to feel the relaxation take over and go deeper and deeper, and still deeper into the muscles and very fiber of your body.

As you become more and more deeply relaxed, your body may feel very heavy. It is also possible that parts of your body may feel very small or maybe even quite large. You may feel warm all over, or perhaps parts of your body have no feeling. For instance, maybe a hand or foot even feels like it is disconnected from the rest of your body. Whatever you feel as you sit there completely relaxed, just go along with it and enjoy it. Let it happen without trying to control or question it. The reason is that these feelings are perfectly natural in a deeply relaxed state. They are normal, for instance, when you are drifting off to sleep. The difference here is that you can let your mind go blank or let your thoughts drift around without going to sleep. Let yourself feel calm and peaceful, warm and relaxed.

The final part of training in relaxation is the most important part because it is concerned with mentally letting go as well as physically relaxing, of getting rid of cares and frustrations and mentally relaxing without going to sleep. To begin, I want you to picture in your mind's eye a scene representing pure, unconditional pleasure to you.

You may want to concentrate on something you've experienced recently, or perhaps you remember something wonderful about a vacation you've taken, or you may recall something you've seen in a movie or read in a book. It is even possible to think of some happy event that may have occurred while you were in the middle of some hectic activity. Of course, you may want to recall something serene or pleasurable from your childhood.

Whatever comes to you, let it be your own private experience to feel fully again for just a little while. Let your mind drift peacefully and relaxed wherever it wants to go. If your mind begins to wander, don't be concerned or fight it. Rather, gently bring your mind back to the scene you have chosen. I am going to remain silent now for a few minutes while you allow yourself to follow anything pleasant, happy, or peaceful that appears to you. Let it take you wherever you want to go, just drifting and enjoying. After a few minutes of silence, I'm going to slowly count from one to five while you bring yourself back to the present, at which time you will awaken yourself, refreshed and calm.

Two minute pause...

Please keep our eyes closed until you are asked to open them. It is now time to come back to the present. You may have been relaxed for so long that it may take a minute or two for you to become fully alert again. This is to be expected at first, but with regular practice you'll find that you can become relaxed very quickly, and that when you have refreshed yourself in this way, you will always be able to arouse yourself effectively by counting from one to five.

This counting will always bring you back from your deep relaxation fully alert and refreshed with all physical exertion and emotional strain gone.

I'll count for you this time. You may wish to count silently to yourself along with me:

1. You are more aware of the present and finding yourself more refreshed and more invigorated than you have ever been in your whole life.

2. It's time to stir about by moving your feet and legs. Remember that when you open your eyes, you will be refreshed as though you were awakening from a long nap.

3. You might want to stretch your arms out from head to foot you are feeling perfect mentally, physically, and emotionally.

4. Now you can move your head around a bit You are now completely refreshed, rejuvenated and ready to open your eyes.

5. Open your eyes.

PASSIVE MUSCLE RELAXATION SCRIPT #1

Start out by taking two or three deep breaths... and let yourself settle back into the chair, the bed, or wherever you happen to be right now... making yourself fully comfortable. Let this be a time just for yourself, putting aside all worries and concerns of the day... and making this a time just for you... letting each part of your body begin to relax... starting with your feet. Just imagine your feet letting go and relaxing right now... letting go of any excess tension in your feet. Just imagine it draining away... and as your feet are relaxing, imagine relaxation moving up into your calves. Let the muscles in your calves unwind and loosen up and let go... allow any tension you're feeling in your calves to just drain away easily and quickly... and as your calves are relaxing, allow relaxation to move up into your thighs... letting the muscles in your thighs unwind and smooth out and relax completely. You might begin to feel your legs from your waist down to your feet becoming more and more relaxed. You might notice your legs becoming heavy as they relax more and more. Continuing now to let the relaxation move into your hips... feeling any excess tension in your hips dissolve and flow away. And soon you might allow relaxation to move into your stomach area... just letting go of any strain or uncomfortableness in your stomach... let it all go right now, imagining deep sensations of relaxation spreading all around your stomach... and continuing to allow the relaxation to move up into your chest. All the muscles in your chest can unwind and loosen up and let go. Each time you exhale, you might imagine breathing away any remaining tension in your chest until your chest feels completely relaxed... and you find it easy to enjoy the good feeling of relaxation as it deepens and develops throughout your chest, stomach area, and your legs. And shortly, you might allow relaxation to move into your shoulders... just letting deep sensations of calmness and relaxation spread all through the muscles of your shoulders... allowing your shoulders to drop... allowing them to feel completely relaxed. And you might now allow the relaxation in your shoulders to move down into your arms, spreading into your upper arms, down into your elbows and forearms, and finally all the way down to your wrists and hands... letting your arms relax... enjoying the good feeling of relaxation in your arms... putting aside any worries, any uncomfortable, unpleasant thoughts right now... letting yourself be totally in the present moment as you let yourself relax more and more. You can feel relaxation moving into your neck now. All the muscles in your neck just unwind, smooth out and relax completely. Just imagine the muscles in your neck loosening up just like a knotted cord being unraveled. And soon, the relaxation can move into your chin and jaws... allowing your jaws to relax... letting your jaws loosen up, and as they are relaxing, you can imagine relaxation moving into the area around your eyes. Any tension around your eyes can just dissipate and flow away as you allow your eyes to relax completely. Any eyestrain just dissolves now and your eyes can fully relax. And you let your forehead relax too... letting the muscles in your forehead smooth out and relax completely... noticing the weight of your head against whatever it's resting on as you allow your entire head to relax completely. Just enjoying the good feeling of relaxation all over now... letting yourself drift deeper and deeper into quietness and peace... getting more and more in touch with that place deep inside of perfect stillness and serenity.

Clyde M. Feldman, Ph.D.

PASSIVE MUSCLE RELAXATION SCRIPT #2

Let your eyes begin to close... and as they close take a deep breath. A deep breath all the way down into your abdomen. Now you can begin to relax every muscle in your body. Let your legs begin to relax... let your legs begin to feel heavy... heavier and heavier as they relax... heavier and heavier as they let go of the last bit of muscular tension. Your legs are becoming more and more heavy and relaxed... like heavy lead pipes. Imagine them as heavy lead pipes... so heavy and relaxed. Your arms too are becoming more and more heavy... heavier and heavier as if they had become heavy lead pipes. You feel gravity pulling them down. You feel your arms letting go of the last bit of muscular tension... letting go... letting go... letting go of tension as they get heavier and heavier, more and more deeply relaxed. Your arms and legs feel heavy, heavy, and relaxed. Your body is relaxing as your arms and legs let go of the last bit of muscular tension. They are totally relaxed, And now your lace begins to relax... your face begins to let go, let go, let go of the tension. Your forehead becomes smooth as silk, smooth as silk... your forehead feels smooth and relaxed, letting go of tension... letting go of all the tensions of the day... letting go of every worry and concern... becoming smooth and relaxed as you let go of any worries from the day. And your cheeks too are becoming relaxed, smooth and relaxed... your cheeks are relaxed and letting go of tension... your forehead and cheeks are totally relaxed and now you begin to relax your jaw... allowing your jaw to become looser and relaxed... loose and relaxed. Your jaw is letting go of tension as you feel the muscles relax and let go of any anger, any frustration from the day. Your jaw is letting go of anger and frustration as you feel your lips begin to part. Your lips will begin to part as you let go of the last bit of tension In your jaw... and as you let go of tension In your jaw your lips begin to part. And now you feel your tongue relax... your tongue is lolling in your mouth... and as your jaw relaxes you feel your neck and shoulders letting go of tension... you feel your neck becoming completely relaxed. There is no tension in your neck as you relax your neck and now your shoulders... your shoulders can begin to droop as you let go of all the anxiety and all concerns. Your shoulders droop and let go of the last bit of muscular tension... letting go, letting go, letting go of all the muscular tension. Your neck and shoulders are totally relaxed. And now you can relax your chest and abdomen by taking a deep breath... a deep breath all the way down into your abdomen... you take a deep breath and it fills your abdomen... and as you let go, the tension goes out of your body with the old air. And now you can take another deep breath into your abdomen... filling your abdomen as you relax your chest and stomach. And as you let go of the old air all the tension goes out of your body and you feel more and more deeply relaxed... your arms and legs heavy and relaxed... your face smooth and relaxed... your jaw loose and relaxed... your neck relaxed, your shoulders drooping... your whole body feeling totally relaxed.

BREATHING TECHNIQUES SCRIPTS

Breathing Awareness

1. Close your eyes. Put your right hand on your abdomen, right at the waistline, and put your left hand on your chest, right in the center.

2. Without trying to change your breathing, simply notice how you are breathing. Which hand rises the most as you inhale- the hand on your chest or the hand on your belly?

If your abdomen expands, then you are breathing from your abdomen or diaphragm. If your belly doesn't move or moves less than your chest then you are breathing from your chest. The trick to shifting from chest to abdomen breathing is to make one or two full exhalations that push out the air from the bottom of your lungs. This will create a vacuum that will pull in a deep, diaphragmatic breath on your next inhalation.

Diaphragmatic or Abdominal Breathing

1. Lie down on a rug or blanket on the floor in a "dead body" pose - your legs straight and slightly apart, your toes pointed comfortably outward, your arms at your sides and not touching your body, your palms up, and your eyes dosed.

2. Bring your attention to your breathing and place your hand on the spot that seems to rise and fall the most as you inhale and exhale.

3. Gently place both of your hands or a book on your abdomen and follow your breathing. Notice how your abdomen rises with each inhalation and falls with each exhalation.

4. Breathe through your nose. (If possible, always clear your nasal passages before doing breathing exercises.)

5. If you experience difficulty breathing into your abdomen, press your hand down on your abdomen as you exhale and let your abdomen push your hand back up as you inhale deeply.

6. Is your chest moving in harmony with your abdomen or is it rigid? Spend a minute or two letting your chest follow the movement of your abdomen

7. If you continue to experience difficulty breathing into your abdomen, an alternative is to lie on your stomach, with your head rested on your folded hands. Take deep abdominal breaths so you can feel your abdomen pushing against the floor.

Breath Training

1. Exhale first. At the first sign of nervousness or panic, at the first "what if" thought that you might pass out, have a heart attack, or be unable to breathe, always exhale. It is important to exhale first so that your lungs open up and it feels like there's plenty of room to take a good deep breath.

2. Inhale and exhale through your nose. Exhaling through your nose will slow down your breathing and prevent hyperventilation. As an alternative to breathing through your nose, inhale through your mouth and make a purifying exhalation through your mouth by pretending that you are blowing out through a straw.

3. Lie on your back with your hand over your abdomen, and the other hand on your chest. Exhale first, and then breathe in through your nose, counting "One... Two... Three." Pause a second, and then breathe out through your mouth, counting "One... Two... Three... Four." Make sure that your exhalation is always longer than your inhalation. This will protect you from taking short, gasping panic breaths.

4. After you feel comfortable with step 3, you can slow your breathing even further. Breathe in and count "One... Two... Three... Four" - pause and breathe out counting "One... Two... Three... Four... Five.". Keep practicing these slow deep breaths, putting the hand on your abdomen up, but allowing very little movement for the hand on your chest. When your minds drifts, refocus on your breathing.

Alternative Positions

1a. Lie on your stomach with your hands folded under your head. Continue to count "One... Two... Three" as you breathe in and "One... Two... Three ... Four" as you breathe out. As in step 4 above, breathe even more slowly by counting to four as you inhale and to five as you exhale.

2a. Step 4 can also be done while you are standing, walking, and sitting. Pace your steps to match the same slow rate of your breathing.

When paced breathing feels comfortable and natural, you can replace counting with the words "in" as you inhale and "calm" as you exhale. Maintain the same pace, making each exhalation last slightly longer than each inhalation. Breathe in through your nose and breathe out through your mouth. Always exhale first.

CREATING A SPECIAL PLACE SCRIPT

A special place might be at the end of a path that leads to a pond. Grass is under your feet, the pond is about 30 yards away and mountains are in the distance. You can feel the coolness of the air in this shady spot. The mockingbird is singing everyone's song. The sun is bright on the pond. The honeysuckle's pungent odor attracts the bee buzzing over the flower with its sweet nectar. Or your special place might be a sparkling clean kitchen, with cinnamon buns baking in the oven. Through the kitchen window you can see fields of yellow wheat. A window chime flutters in the breeze. At the table is a cup of tea for your guest. Try recording this exercise and playing it, or have a friend read it to you slowly.

To go to your safe place, lie down, be totally comfortable. Close your eyes...Walk slowly to a quiet place in your mind... Your place can be inside or outside ... It needs to be peaceful and safe... Picture yourself unloading your anxieties, your worries... Notice the view in the distance... What do you smell?... What do you hear?... Notice what is before you... Reach out and touch it... How does it feel?... Smell it... Hear it... Make the temperature comfortable... Be safe here ... Look around for a special spot, a private spot... Find the path to this place... Feel the ground with your feet... Look above you... What do you see? ... Hear?... Smell?... Walk down this path until you can enter your own quiet, comfortable, safe place.

You have arrived at your special place... What is under your feet?... How does it feel?... Take several steps... What do you see above you?... What do you hear?... Do you hear something else?... Reach and touch something... What is its texture?... are there pens, paper, paint nearby, or is there sand to draw in, clay to work?... Go to them, handle them, smell them. These are your special tools, or tools for your inner guide to reveal ideas or feelings to you... Look as far as you can see... What do you see?... What do you hear?... What aromas do you notice?

Now you need to find a place for your inner guide and a path from which your guide can enter. Sit or lie down in your special place... Notice its smells, sounds, sights...This is your place and nothing can harm you here... If danger is here, expel it... Spend three to five minutes realizing you are relaxed, safe and comfortable.

Memorize this place's smells, tastes, sights, sounds... You can come back and relax here whenever you want... Leave by the same path or entrance... Notice the ground, touch things near you... Look far away and appreciate the view... Remind yourself this special place you created can be entered whenever you wish. Say an affirmation such as, "I can relax here," or "This is my special place. I can come here whenever I wish." Now open your eyes and spend a few seconds appreciating your relaxation.

BEACH AND FOREST SPECIAL PLACES SCRIPTS

The Beach

You're walking down a long wooden stairway to a very beautiful, expansive beach. It looks almost deserted and stretches off into the distance as far as you can see. The sand is very fine and light... almost white in appearance. You step onto the sand in your bare feet and rub it between your toes. It feels so good to walk slowly along this beautiful beach. The roaring sound of the surf is so soothing that you can just let go of anything on your mind. You're watching the waves ebb and flow... they are slowly coming in... breaking over each other... and then slowly flowing back out again. The ocean itself is a very beautiful shade of blue... a shade of blue that is so relaxing just to look at. You look out over the surface of the ocean all the way to the horizon, and then follow the horizon as far as you can see, noticing how it bends slightly downward as it follows the curvature of the earth. As you scan the ocean you can see, many miles offshore, a tiny sailboat skimming along the surface of the water. And all these sights help you to just let go and relax even more. As you continue walking down the beach, you become aware of the fresh, salty smell of the sea air. You take in a deep breath... breathe out... and feel very refreshed and even more relaxed. Overhead you notice two seagulls flying out to sea... looking very graceful as they soar into the wind... and you imagine how you might feel yourself if you had the freedom to fly. You find yourself settling into a deep state of relaxation as you continue walking down the beach. You feel the sea breeze blowing gently against your cheek and the warmth of the sun overhead penetrating your neck and shoulders. The warm, liquid sensation of the sun just relaxes you even more... and you're beginning to feel perfectly content on this beautiful beach. It's such a lovely day. In a moment, up ahead, you see a comfortable looking beach chair. Slowly, you begin to approach the beach chair... and when you finally reach it, you sit back and settle in. Laying back in this comfortable beach chair, you let go and relax even more, drifting even deeper into relaxation. In a little while you might close your eyes and just listen to the sound of the surf, the unending cycle of waves ebbing and flowing. And the rhythmic sound of the surf carries you even deeper... deeper still... into a wonderful state of quietness and peace.

The Forest

You're walking along a path deep in the forest. All around you there are tall trees... pine, fir, redwood, oak... try to see them. The rushing sound of the wind blowing through the treetops is so soothing, allowing you to let go. You can smell the rich dampness of the forest floor, the smell of earth and new seedlings and rotting leaves. Now you look up through the treetops until you can see a light blue sky. You notice how high the sun is in the sky. As the sun enters the canopy of the treetops, it breaks into rays which waft their way down through the trees to the forest floor. You're watching the intricate patterns of light and shadow created as the light filters down through the trees. The forest feels like a great primeval cathedral ... filling you with a sense of peace and reverence for all living things. Off in the distance, you can hear the sound of rushing water echoing through the forest. It gets louder as you approach, and before long you are at the edge of a mountain stream. You're looking at the stream, noticing how clear and sparkling the water is. Imagine sitting down and making yourself very comfortable. You might sit down on a flat rock up against a tree or you might even decide to lay down on a grassy slope. You can see the mountain stream creating rapids as it moves, rushing around a variety of large and small rocks. These rocks are many shades of brown, gray, and white and some are covered with moss. You can see the sparkling water rushing over some and around others, making whirlpools and eddies. The rushing sound of the water is so peaceful that you can just let yourself drift... relaxing more and more. You take in a deep breath of fresh air and breathe out, finding the subtle smells of the forest very refreshing. As you let yourself sink into the soft bed of grass or dead leaves or fragrant pine needles beneath you, you can let go of any strains or concerns... allowing the sights, sounds, and smells of this beautiful wooded area to fill you with a deep sense of peace.

16 THINGS TO ASK YOURSELF ABOUT YOUR THOUGHTS, BELIEFS, ASSUMPTIONS AND EXPECTATIONS

(TO HELP CREATE NEW ONES)

1. What's the hard evidence for this being true? Have you really tested it out fully or did you just decide to <u>accept</u> it as true?

2. Does this hold true 100% of the time and in 100% of situations?

3. Do others agree with what you say to yourself and think it's healthy?

4. Has this always been true? Have you ever done anything in your life that was an exception to this or that contradicted this?

5. Is what you say to yourself flexible, have exceptions, and have grey areas or is it totally black & white, rigid, with no exceptions?

6. Who says? Compared to what? Compared to who? Based on what standard? Who decided that standard?

7. Is believing this good for you? Does it make you feel <u>better</u> about yourself, more in <u>control</u> of your life, better able to <u>cope</u> -or- does it make you feel worse, less in control, and less able to cope?

8. Does this keep you focused on the big picture, or does it keep you focused on one narrow aspect of things... like tunnel vision?

9. Do this make you <u>over</u>-emphasize and exaggerate the negative things and make you <u>under</u>-emphasize and minimize the positive things?

10. Is your rational, logical, and objective side telling you this -or- is it all based on intense feelings and emotions?

11. Is this something you <u>decided</u> to think and believe on your own, or did you get it from the past or from people like parents, etc.?

12. If you had a best friend in your situation, would you take the same attitude about <u>them</u> and <u>their situation</u> that you do about <u>yours</u>?

13. Image someone who's more like the way you <u>wish</u> you could be? Would <u>they</u> be saying the same things to themself as you do?

14. If you could magically get rid of this or take it less personally and less seriously, what would you be able to do, to feel, to believe, and to handle that you can't now?

15. What's the <u>worst</u> that could actually happen and how likely is that?

16. What would happen if you could stop saying this to yourself?
    Who's stopping you?

POSITIVE COUNTER-STATEMENTS AND PICTURES WORKSHEET FOR REDUCING ANXIETY

YOUR ANXIOUS, FEARFUL, CATASTROPHIC THOUGHTS, BELIEFS, ASSUMPTIONS, EXPECTATIONS, AND PICTURES:

1a. _____

2a. _____

3a. _____

4a. _____

YOUR POSITIVE COUNTER-STATEMENTS, POSITIVE COPING STATEMENTS, AND POSITIVE MENTAL PICTURES FOR EACH OF THE ABOVE:

1b. _____

2b. _____

3b. _____

4b. _____

Clyde M. Feldman, Ph.D.

GRADED HIERARCHY

THINK OF AN ANXIETY PRODUCING SITUATION (social situation, panic attack situation, worry situation, feared place/object, or traumatic trigger, etc.). BREAK IT DOWN INTO 8-20 SMALLER PIECES OR PARTS, WITH THE FIRST ONE BEING THE EASIEST TO HANDLE AND THE LEAST ANXIETY PRODUCING. THE NEXT ONES WILL EACH BE A LITTLE MORE CHALLENGING AND ANXIETY PRODUCING.

1. _____

2. _____

3. _____

4. _____

5. _____

6. _____

7. _____

8. _____

9. _____

10. _____

11. _____

12. _____

13. _____

14. _____

15. _____

16. _____

17. _____

18. _____

19. _____

20. _____

SECTION 4:

BOOK REFERENCES ON EXPOSURE THERAPY

Barlow, D.H., & Cerny, J.A. (1988). *Psychological Treatment of Panic*. New York: Gilford Press.

Barlow, D.H., & Craske, M.G. (2000). *Master of Your Anxiety and Panic: Client Workbook for Anxiety and Panic*. Greywind.

Beck, A.T., Emery, G., & Greenberg, R.L. (1985). *Anxiety Disorders and Phobias*. Basic Books.

Berstein, D.A., & Borkovec, T.D. (1973). *Progressive Relaxation Training*. Research Press.

Bourne, E.J. (1998). *Overcoming Specific Phobia: Therapist Protocol*. Oakland: New Harbinger.

Bourne, E.J. (2000). *The Anxiety & Phobia Workbook*. Oakland: New Harbinger.

Craske, M.G., Barlow, D.H., & Meadows, E.A. (2000). *Mastery of Your Anxiety and Panic: Therapist Guide for Anxiety, Panic, and Agoraphobia*. Greywind.

Craske, M.G., Barlow, D.H., & O'Leary, T.A. (1992). *Mastery of Your Anxiety and Worry: Client Workbook*. Oxford: Oxford University Press.

Leahy, R.L., & Holland, S.J. (2000). *Treatment Plans and Interventions for Depression and Anxiety Disorders*. New York: Guildford Press.

Smyth, L.D. (1999). *Clinician's Manual for the Cognitive-Behavioral Treatment of Post Traumatic Stress Disorder*. Baltimore: Red Toad Road.

Smyth, L.D. (1999). *Client's Manual for the Cognitive-Behavioral Treatment of the Anxiety Disorders*. Baltimore: Red Toad Road.

White, J. (1999). *Overcoming Generalized Anxiety Disorder: Therapist Protocol*. Oakland: New Harbinger.

Wolpe, J. (1988). *Life Without Fear*. Oakland: New Harbinger.

Zinbarg, R.E., Craske, M.G., & Barlow, D.H. (1993). *Mastery of Your Anxiety and Worry*. Greywind.

Made in the USA
Lexington, KY
22 April 2015